THE ART OF ACCOMPANIMENT

Four essential conversations on becoming
the kind of parish the church needs today

BILL HUEBSCH

TWENTY-THIRD
PUBLICATIONS
twentythirdpublications.com

SECOND PRINTING 2017

TWENTY-THIRD PUBLICATIONS
A division of Bayard
One Montauk Avenue, Suite 200
New London, CT 06320
(860) 437-3012 or (800) 321-0411
www.twentythirdpublications.com

Cover Photo: M.MIGLIORATO/CPP/CIRIC

ISBN: 978-1-62785-262-3

Printed in the U.S.A.

A division of Bayard, Inc.

How to use this resource

STUDY

This booklet provides a guide to four conversations designed to help pastoral leaders understand, plan for, and become an accompanying parish. It is also suited to individual use. If used alone, simply read through each statement: pray the prayers, reflect on the content, and think through the discussion questions. If used as a group, we recommend you gather your group and begin with the prayer we provide. Then move around the circle in your group and read aloud the numbered statements, rotating readers with each stanza. Group members should note items that strike them as especially important and return to them during the discussion periods.

CONVERSATION AND PRAYER

When you come to the prayer and group process notes, continue around the circle discussing or praying as the notes direct. Use our suggestions as a starting point and add your own questions, prayers, or action plans. The group may also pause anywhere along the line to discuss the content.

FOUR CONVERSATIONS ABOUT ACCOMPANIMENT

Each conversation opens with a brief shared prayer

CONVERSATION ONE

Accompaniment as a Pastoral Strategy

- An introduction and three principles

- Introduction: The church needs accompanists

- Principle #1: Accompaniment is a sacred task

- Principle #2: Grace is the force behind accompaniment

- Principle #3: We have reverence for the divine mystery in each other

CONVERSATION TWO

Accompaniment in the Formation of the Conscience

Five principles leading to the wisdom of Jesus

- Principle #1: God speaks to us in the depths of our conscience

- Principle #2: We accompany people to help them hear God

- Principle #3: Avoid being overly church-law-centered

- Principle #4: Avoid being overly self-centered

- Principle #5: Seek to be well-balanced and Christ-centered

CONVERSATION THREE

Accompaniment toward Discernment

An introduction and four principles

- Introduction: Listening deeply for the voice of Jesus

- Principle #1: Discernment deals with practical, life-changing questions

- Principle #2: Discernment is couched in prayer

- Principle #3: Discernment eventually leads to a discussion of the matter

- Principle #4: Good decisions made in discernment lead to consolation

CONVERSATION FOUR
Hallmarks of an "Accompanying Parish"
Nine hallmarks for use in pastoral planning

- Hallmark #1: The parish priest and pastoral team are committed to accompaniment

- Hallmark #2: The parish team plans for ways to increase accompaniment

- Hallmark #3: Mercy for people's life situations is obvious and generous

- Hallmark #4: Families are accompanied in the religious education programs

- Hallmark #5: Everyone is accompanied through the Sunday liturgy

- Hallmark #6: Pastoral care ministries are "accompaniment specialists"

- Hallmark #7: The "voice" of the parish is consistently companionable

- Hallmark #8: The parish respects that people gradually become fully faithful

- Hallmark #9: The parish reaches out beyond its comfort zone

Accompaniment as a pastoral strategy

AN INTRODUCTION AND THREE PRINCIPLES

PRAYER
Become aware of the presence of God

ALL: In the name of the Father, and of the Son,
and of the Holy Spirit. Amen.

[1] Jesus accompanies us through each day as a shepherd does the sheep. Jesus walks beside us aware of our needs and desires, tending us gently. The Holy Spirit guides us and opens our hearts to hear the word and live by it. God fills the world with the fragrance of Christ, now flowing through us as we accompany each other to new life.

[2] "But thanks be to God, who in Christ always leads us in triumphal procession, and through us spreads in every place the fragrance that comes from knowing him. For we are the aroma of Christ to God among those who are being saved and among those who are perishing; to the one a fragrance from death to death, to the other a fragrance from life to life" (2 Corinthians 2:14–16a, NRSV).

[3] Let us become consciously aware now of this ever-present God, allowing our hearts to swell with the experience of the divine presence. Allow the fragrance of Christ to fill your senses. Let his gaze of love for

you fall upon you. What is this experience of being near to God like for you? *(Brief sacred pause, followed by sharing.)*

[4] O God, we know that you are with us, and that you accompany us in all that we do. We open our hearts to your love. Grant that, by the light of your Holy Spirit, we may be humble as we walk with others and charitable in all that we do here today. We pray through Christ, our Lord.

ALL: Amen.

INTRODUCTION
The Church needs accompanists

[5] "In our world," Pope Francis teaches us, "ordained ministers and other pastoral workers can make present the fragrance of Christ's closeness and his personal gaze. The Church will have to initiate everyone—priests, religious and laity—into this 'art of accompaniment' which teaches us to remove our sandals before the sacred ground of the other" (*The Joy of the Gospel*, 169).

[6] With these words Pope Francis has called us all to understand how to accompany others and how to make such accompaniment part of our pastoral practice in every parish. Learning this art and putting it into practice is the purpose of these four conversations. As we talk together about this, we grow together as accompanists. Let us bring our hearts and souls into these conversations in order to make present the fragrance of Christ to those who need it most.

[7] For many in pastoral ministry, this will come quite naturally and be a welcome affirmation of how they have always done their work. For others, this will be somewhat new and challenging in their ministry. Pope Francis is asking us to have deep reverence for the experiences of others. We may not understand or identify with someone who has, for example,

left the church for decades and now wants to return, or someone who is living in a second marriage and cannot ask for an annulment, or someone who is at odds with church teaching on contraception. But Pope Francis teaches us that, as accompanists, our task is to listen and guide but not to judge and condemn.

[8] But first, what exactly is accompaniment? How do we become an "accompanying parish"? To most of us this is a new term when applied to pastoral ministry. We are accustomed to hearing about "accompanists" but we think of them as piano players who accompany singers. What do we mean when we use this term to describe the art of accompaniment when it applies to each other as Christians on a lifelong journey to the heart of Christ?

[9] The metaphor of the piano player is actually quite a good one. A musical accompanist is somewhat in the background of the performance, allowing the singer to shine. It is the singer who sets the stage and who determines the phrasing and tempo of the song. The role of the accompanist is to help the singer stay on tune and to embellish the singer's performance with stunning beauty.

[10] Accompanists often sit in the shadow of the great voices of these great singers. Being the pianist who plays for them can feel like the most thankless job in music. The singers couldn't do it without them but it's the sopranos and the tenors who get all the glory, as well as most of the cash and applause. It's all about the singer on stage; the accompanists, meanwhile, are busy playing fiendishly difficult accompaniments by Schubert or Schumann.

[11] It's very similar for pastoral ministers who accompany persons through the ups and downs of life and faith. As accompanists, we learn to allow the parishioner being accompanied to shine. Each person is "making their own kind of music," and our role is to help them do it well. We make use of the tools given to us by the church to offer them

guidance, but in the end, the conscience of the one being accompanied must be allowed to set the stage. Their timing (and it may take many years in some cases) is our timing.

[12] Ours is not to choose the song, not to set the tempo, and not to dominate the conversation. We can coach them into quiet times of prayer as a way of helping them be in touch with what God is calling them to, but in the end, the mystery of God's grace in their lives is not for us to direct. As accompanists, we need few words; we must be careful not to numb the one being accompanied by our sermons and explanations.

[13] To accompany another Christian on the journey of faith requires first and foremost as pastoral leaders that our own hearts be in Christ. We become the hands and feet, the voice and gaze, *the very fragrance* of Christ for one another. How can we accompany someone else to accept God's desire for them if we ourselves are not reflecting God's desire for us in our own lives?

IN YOUR OWN WORDS (DISCUSSION TIME)

[14] Therefore, we who would accompany others must be accompanied by someone ourselves. Who accompanies you? Looking back over your life, who are the people who have appeared at the right moment to accompany you so that you could become your most real self? When have you experienced a dearth of accompaniment, a time when you needed encouragement and assistance but were not offered it?

[15] Likewise, how has the word of God accompanied you? How has the church through her sacraments and people been your companion and guide? In your life today, to whom do you turn in those moments when you most need the companionship that assures you; challenges what you think, do, or fail to do; and tells you the truth?

PRINCIPLE #1
Accompaniment is a sacred task

[16] To accompany others is a sacred task but one that occurs in our daily lives very often. We walk with one another day in and day out. Parents with their children. Spouses with each other. Friends, colleagues, teachers, neighbors, and even strangers may appear in our lives as companions.

[17] This daily "walking with" becomes "accompaniment" only when we lead others ever closer to the heart of God. If all we do with others all day is "chatter," then we are merely standing side by side without that all-important common, inner force that is the Spirit. Our task as accompanists is not to affirm everything in each other's lives, but to invite each other to the freedom of God. This means that we invite each other to follow the pathway of love and joy that leads us, deeply and truly, to become the persons God creates us to be.

[18] Without this orientation toward the desire of God for us, we quickly become drifters in a world lacking meaning. We become spiritually homeless. Walking with each other without calling one another to the heart of God is counterproductive. It's a sort of self-absorbed therapy, but it is not a pilgrimage to the Father (*The Joy of the Gospel*, 170).

[19] Therefore, we can say that to accompany another is more than merely "to walk with him or her." Accompaniment is more intimate and intentional; it's more dynamic and life-changing. The word "accompany" itself suggests this intimacy. Its literal meaning might be rendered as "to break bread with another..." We become companions, trusted and known. Pope Francis reminds us to "remove our sandals" with reverence —for the personal journey we witness when we accompany another is indeed a glance at the face of God.

[20] In today's church, Pope Francis tells us, we need men and women who, on the basis of their experience of accompanying others, know how

prudence, understanding, patience, and docility to the Spirit play a role in leading others closer to Christ. One who accompanies others must be willing to wait for the Spirit to move in the heart of the other. Without the Spirit, any imposed set of rules or laws, even if they come from the church, will fall on deaf ears, leaving the one being accompanied with anger and hurt and the accompanist feeling frustrated (*The Joy of the Gospel*, 171).

PRINCIPLE #2
Grace is the force behind accompaniment

[21] One who accompanies another must always cooperate with grace. Grace is enough for us. Without grace, we are powerless.

[22] Grace is a free gift from God who loves us unconditionally. It is God giving us God's own very self in a radical and real way, empowering us to become the persons we are created to be. In this relationship of love offered to us by God, we find ourselves saying, "I am a sinner whom the Lord looked upon with mercy" (Pope Francis in an interview, December 2, 2015). This grace is given to us even as we live in our individual situations in life, experiencing our own spiritual journeys (*Catechism of the Catholic Church*, 1999).

[23] Grace is a personal communication from God. It elaborates the relationship between God and us in a profound way. It is like a force or sacred power that fills us. Through grace we are enthused for love, empowered to work for justice, and able to become the richly gifted persons God desires us to become.

[24] Spiritual accompaniment operates in the realm of grace. Grace gives accompaniment its force. We might say, then, that accompaniment is "help given by one Christian to another which enables that person to pay attention to God's personal communication to him or her [that is,

to *the force of grace*], to respond to this personally communicating God, and to live out of the consequence of the relationship" (William Barry, SJ, and William Connolly, SJ. *The Practice of Spiritual Direction*. San Francisco: HarperOne, 2009).

[25] And what exactly is "the consequence" of being related to God or of receiving grace? It is to be oriented to the heart of the Lord. Even during a busy day or in the middle of the night, we find ourselves mindful of the presence of God. This becomes our compass; everything in our life is directed by it.

[26] And even more, the consequence of being given grace is that we begin to realize, ever so slowly at first, that God loves us. God has forgiven us even if we have not forgiven ourselves, even if other people or the church itself has failed to forgive us. This is where real faith is needed. Do you believe that God has forgiven you and still loves you, even as a sinner?

[27] "No one can be condemned forever," Pope Francis reminds us, "because that is not the logic of the Gospel!" (*The Joy of Love*, 297). "The way of the Church is not to condemn anyone forever; it is to pour out the balm of God's mercy on all those who ask for it with a sincere heart" (homily at Mass celebrated with the new cardinals, 15 February, 2015).

[28] Thus, in spiritual accompaniment we are guiding each other along the pathway of God. We extend to one another the unbelievable and life-changing truth that we have seen; and the truth is that God forgives us completely. Accompaniment also leads us to become God-like. We call each other to be more forgiving, more generous, less judgmental, less greedy, more loving, more enthused, less harsh, less full of lust, and closer to the heart of Jesus.

IN YOUR OWN WORDS (DISCUSSION TIME)
[29] Go back over the section we just read and in your own words describe what it means to accompany someone, cooperating with grace

in their lives. Think about the families and individuals in your parish, including those who are absent from regular parish life. How can the parish and you as pastoral ministers better accompany them at times like baptism, religious education, preparation for a child's first sacraments, illness, family planning questions, the dying process, or whatever marriage situation they live in?

PRINCIPLE #3
We have reverence for the divine mystery in each other

[30] No one can plumb the mystery of God's presence in the life of another person. Therefore, we must listen carefully to how God calls each person to himself (*The Joy of the Gospel*, 171). It goes without saying then that we who accompany others must learn the art of listening, which is more than simply hearing. To listen is to have an open heart; this leads to genuine encounter and intimacy in Christ.

[31] A good accompanist can also find the right gesture and word in just the right moment when it is time to speak, offering the one being accompanied a gentle nudge toward God's heart. For we are more than mere bystanders, watching each other from a distance but saying nothing in the face of evil and darkness. We are also more than mere judges, lording it over others as though only we have the right answers for everyone in every situation.

[32] It is in this middle ground—between saying nothing and rendering harsh judgments—that accompaniment flourishes. An accompanist has his or her heart tuned into the flow of grace, of God's love for us, God's willingness to forgive even the most serious offenses. The accompanist listens to both God and the one being accompanied and draws them together with the gentle love of the father who was awaiting the return of his prodigal son, arms open, heart ready, reflecting the face of God's love.

[33] One who accompanies others must realize that each person's relationship with God is a mystery. God calls us in ways that often surprise us and may not be fully understood. A spiritual accompanist, therefore, is not an intrusive judge who scolds and condemns but a companion who has reverence for the mysterious ways in which God may be working in the life of the other (*The Joy of the Gospel*, 172).

[34] A well-trained accompanist "invites others to let themselves be healed, to take up their mat, embrace the cross, leave all behind, and go forth ever anew" (*The Joy of the Gospel*, 172). We learn as accompanists to be patient and compassionate with others, as we hope they will be with us.

IN YOUR OWN WORDS (DISCUSSION TIME)

[35] What is your experience of accompanying others? How have you learned this art? Without betraying the confidence of anyone in the parish, take all the time you need at this point to share some stories of accompaniment.

Accompaniment in the Formation of the Conscience

SIX PRINCIPLES LEADING TO THE WISDOM OF JESUS

PRAYER

Center ourselves in the presence of Christ

ALL: In the name of the Father, and of the Son,
and of the Holy Spirit. Amen.

[1] God speaks to us in the depths of our conscience. We must become attuned to God's voice sounding in our hearts. But understanding God's voice is never something we do alone. We are a people, a community formed around the Word, gathered with each other as church.

[2] Let us become aware of God's voice in our own hearts now as we begin this conversation. Pause to remember the past day or two. In what ways has God's gentle and often wordless voice echoed in your heart and soul? In these past days, how have you been called to forgive, be generous, defend the powerless, or speak a word of love in the face of anger, fear, or aggression? *(Brief sacred pause, followed by sharing.)*

[3] O God, we know that you are with us and that you speak in the depths of our hearts. Now grant that, by the light of the Holy Spirit, we

may be more attuned to hearing your voice and ready to follow your way of love. We pray through Christ, our Lord.

ALL: Amen.

God speaks to us in the depths of our conscience

[4] "In the depths of our conscience, we detect a law which we have not laid upon ourselves but which we must obey. Its voice, ever calling us to love and to do what is good and avoid evil, is heard at the right moments in our lives. It speaks to our hearts: 'Do this; shun that.' For this law, written into our very hearts, is from God.

[5] "Our very dignity comes from observing this inner law, and by it we will be judged. Conscience is our most secret core and sanctuary. It is where we are alone with God, whose voice echoes in our depths" (The Constitution on the Church in the Modern World, 16. *Vatican II in Plain English*. Ave Maria Press, 1996).

[6] With these words, the Second Vatican Council describes for us a chief goal of all accompaniment. We Christians seek to help one another discern the voice of God as it echoes in the depths of our souls. To what is God calling us? How can we know?

[7] The *Catechism of the Catholic Church* picked this up in article 1776, where it quotes this section from Vatican II verbatim. Our consciences are our deepest inner sanctuaries where we find our truest selves, the *Catechism* suggests. They are that place where God reveals our destiny and purpose, our most private self, and our divine legacy.

[8] The conscience is more than a court room where we judge right from wrong. It is also and mainly the arena in which we make choices

and learn to follow the pathway that leads us to become more and more the loving persons God has created us to be. Note that in our conscience it is *God* who speaks to us, not the church, not our spouse, not even ourselves. We hear the voice of God as God gives us his own very self as grace, which is the force that moves and shapes us.

IN YOUR OWN WORDS (DISCUSSION TIME)

[9] In general, what are the questions that arise most often in your conscience? What are the thorniest questions facing modern men and women in the culture of your community? What forces in our culture and society make forming one's conscience difficult? How can accompaniment offer the force of grace to lead others to Christ?

PRINCIPLE #2
We accompany people to help them hear God

[10] Our conscience is the place where church teaching meets our own human experience in a sacred dialogue. Here is where God speaks most clearly and distinctly because our conscience is the place where the divine voice defines us. The unique word each of us is, the single word God wishes to speak to the world through us, is articulated in the conscience of each.

[11] Cardinal Blase Cupich speaks about this in one of his columns in *Catholic New World*, the newspaper in the Archdiocese of Chicago (Sept 4, 2016). The term "examination of conscience" has often been portrayed as making a check list of our sins, he says. But there is a much richer approach to examining our conscience, and that is to treat such a meditation as a way to discern the will of God. Such a reflection would be marked "by an openness to how God is calling each of us in our particular circumstances, not only to correct our sinfulness—which we must do—but also to strike out on new paths with a sense of wonder about our lives."

[12] So an authentic accompaniment toward discernment, he says, must involve questions such as, "How and when have I experienced God's grace and call in moments of loss, accomplishment, sinfulness, and reconciliation? What have I learned about myself? What good habits and virtues have I acquired in those experiences? What weaknesses have I struggled to overcome on my own because I have not allowed God's grace to heal them?"

[13] In the sacrament of reconciliation, such a line of inquiry and conversation can help lead people to broaden their understanding of what God may be calling them to do or become. In this way, this sacrament becomes part of the art of accompaniment.

[14] Learning to listen to one's conscience, then, is a principal outcome of all accompaniment. This is a lifelong task for all men and women of good will and one for which we depend upon the church for guidance. As we learn to listen to our conscience, however, we must avoid the temptation to move to either of two dangerous extremes in our thinking.

PRINCIPLE #3
Avoid being overly church-law-centered

[15] On the one extreme, we find those who believe that the only way to understand one's conscience is in light of church law. The law is seen on this extreme as absolute; everyone is expected to align his or her conscience to it as though every human situation is the same and calls for one and the same outcome in discerning one's conscience. "The church knows what is best for you," these might say.

[16] This approach suggests that no one in good faith may ever vary from church law and that to do so is to live in serious sin. It is an overly church-law-centered approach to forming the conscience; it suggests that we are called to holiness by the church rather than by God. Those

on this extreme hold that we are only allowed to form our conscience if we are in accord with literal church teaching.

[17] The church, of course, always holds up the ideal of its laws and asks people to try very hard to meet that ideal. But as the Synod on the Family in 2014 pointed out in article 28, "the church must accompany with attention and care the weakest of her children, who show signs of a wounded and troubled love, by restoring in them hope and confidence, like the beacon of a lighthouse in a port or a torch carried among the people to enlighten those who have lost their way or who are in the midst of a storm."

[18] To those of his day who wanted to be overly centered on church law Jesus offered a warning: Woe to you church-law-keepers, he said in essence. You load people down with legal burdens insisting that they follow the letter of the law which is very difficult to do, and you don't lift a finger to help them through the difficulties of their lives (Luke 11:46).

[19] Woe to you law-keepers. You have taken away the key of inner wisdom and knowledge from people. You don't have this wisdom yourselves and you prevent others from having it too (Luke 11:52).

[20] "But woe to you, scribes and Pharisees, hypocrites! For you lock people out of the kingdom of heaven. For you do not go in yourselves, and when others are going in, you stop them" (Matthew 23:13, NRSV).

[21] "Let us not forget," Pope Francis reminds us, "that the Church's task is often like that of a field hospital" (*The Joy of Love*, 291). The church-law-centered approach to forming the conscience may fail to take into account the wounds of the people of God.

[22] As the final report of the Synod on the Family in 2015 teaches in article 51, there is a need "to avoid judgments which do not take into account the complexity of various situations" and "to be attentive, by

necessity, to how people experience distress because of their condition." An overly church-law-centered understanding of how to understand one's conscience may leave behind many who are suffering through the storms of their lives.

[23] Pope Francis appreciates the good spirit and good will expressed by people holding this church-law-oriented point of view. They want to see strong discipline in the church. But the discipline Pope Francis is calling for aims at forming disciples and not just enforcing rules.

[24] Pope Francis asks us to respect how a person matures in freedom. He wants to see an approach to law and rule that is based on the Catholic tradition rather than on a legalism that simply considers "whether or not an individual's actions correspond to a general law or rule, because that is not enough to discern and ensure full fidelity to God in the concrete life of a human being," as the Holy Father observes (*The Joy of Love*, 304).

IN YOUR OWN WORDS (DISCUSSION TIME)
[25] What is your response to this point of view? What is your experience of it in your own life? How has this approach affected other members of the parish?

PRINCIPLE #4
Avoid being overly self-centered

[26] On the other extreme, we find those who are not church- or law-oriented at all and might even be called "lawless" in how they want to understand the conscience. This is a much more *self*-centered approach. These often believe that, whatever one's desire or whim, one should do as one pleases without regard for church law or community standards. Such a lawless approach results in an "everything goes" mentality that is contrary to our tradition, to the teachings of Jesus, and to good common sense.

[27] One danger of this self-centered approach is the real likelihood that we may simply fool ourselves into justifying pretty much anything we wish to do. Those on this extreme make themselves the center of their choices. They trust mainly in their own way of thinking without need for accompaniment of any kind. "I know what's best for me," these might say.

[28] When we accompany another Christian, we must be sure that our hearts are with the church and its ideals even as we help them sort out the circumstances in their particular lives. We cannot coach people to willy-nilly reject church teaching simply because it does not allow them to do what they wish. Accompaniment is much more oriented toward discerning what God desires for each, and the church is our guide in that discernment, not our enemy.

[29] So accompaniment toward discernment of conscience isn't a matter of yes or no about church teaching but a matter of how a person can best strive toward the church's ideal while still living in and working through the real situation of his or her life.

[30] The goal of accompaniment is not to help people center on themselves. It is not to provide people with a rationale or justification to become independent of the church and its guidance and teachings. The movement toward a genuine acceptance of oneself—which is one goal of accompaniment—never has selfishness as the goal; to be authentically human is to be self-giving, which is to become what God has created us to be; we don't create ourselves.

[31] Furthermore, genuine Christian accompaniment has Christ as its goal. We seek to help people move closer to the heart of the Lord, the sacred heart of Jesus. We want them to pray—that is, to listen closely as the Lord speaks in the depths of their souls, to discern the Lord's voice amid the din of modern temptations and allurements.

[32] To those who would be overly centered on selfishness, Jesus likewise offered a warning. "If any want to become my followers, let them deny themselves and take up their cross daily and follow me. For those who want to save their life will lose it, and those who lose their life for my sake will save it. What does it profit them if they gain the whole world, but lose or forfeit themselves?" (Luke 9:23–25, NRSV).

[33] Taking up the cross of Christ leads only to self-giving love and never to self-centered choices. "Thanks solely to this encounter—or renewed encounter—with God's love, which blossoms into an enriching friendship, we are liberated from our narrowness and self-absorption" (*The Joy of the Gospel*, 8).

IN YOUR OWN WORDS (DISCUSSION TIME)
[34] How do you see this self-centered approach playing out in modern life? What is your personal experience of this approach? How does this affect the people of your parish, especially young people?

PRINCIPLE #5
Seek to be well-balanced and Christ-centered

[35] Therefore, we can say that in between these two extremes—the overly church-law-centered and overly self-centered—is a way that is much more Catholic in tone and approach, a Christ-centered approach. It is outlined for us in the *Catechism* and demonstrates why spiritual accompaniment is so important. How the *Catechism* teaches us to discern our consciences in article 1785 is very much in continuity with long-standing Catholic tradition.

[36] Jesus attuned his conscience to his Father. He heard God's voice and followed it even when that led him to Calvary. Jesus was not on a

remote control from God; he was fully human and took decisions within his conscience. But he wasn't alone; he always acted in concert with his Father.

[37] Jesus made his decisions freely, and he wants that same freedom for us. He wants neither selfish Christians who follow only their own ego, nor weak Christians who are remote-controlled by the church. "Jesus wants us free. And where is this freedom created? It is created in dialogue with God in the person's own conscience" (Pope Francis, *Angelus* on June 30, 2013).

[38] As we think about how Jesus coached and taught his disciples and the people of his time, we see the primordial example of an accompanist. He became a companion to his followers, teaching in ways they could understand, nudging and encouraging them along the way, helping them grasp the most difficult teachings, and doing it all with great love.

[39] He was likewise accompanied by them; Jesus asked his disciples and friends, including many women, to accompany and stay with him. In one famous case, Jesus and his entourage were walking north toward Caesarea Philippi, an ancient Roman town north of the Sea of Galilee. As they walked and talked together, Jesus turned to his disciples to ask one of the most personal and pithy questions in the gospels. What are people saying about me? he asked them. "Who do people say that I am?" (Mark 8:27–30, NRSV).

[40] This question seemed to come straight out of his conscience as he sorted out the will of God in his life. And on that lonely road and dusty day with Jesus, Peter answered on behalf of us all. "You are the Christ," he said. We believe that you are the Messiah. Accompaniment, indeed.

[41] In accompaniment, we grow capable of this Christ-centered approach through prayer, regular participation in the sacramental life of the church, and quiet times scattered throughout our days and nights.

Christ stands beside us at all times, and when we turn our gaze toward him, he opens our ears so we can hear and our eyes to see more clearly.

[42] Our ongoing prayer conversation with Christ allows us to hear his call to us to become more his disciple—that is, more forgiving, generous, and virtuous. We also hear his words of gentle forgiveness and desire that we sin no more. "Neither do I condemn you," he tells us just as he did the woman in the story in John 8:11. And we also hear him thank us for our work, affirm us for our gifts, and laugh with us when things go in unexpected directions.

[43] Christ, of course, is the head of the body that is the church. In and through the ministry of the church, we are able to share our journeys of faith, be guided by the authoritative teachings we find there, and walk together.

IN YOUR OWN WORDS (DISCUSSION TIME)
[44] How do you see this Christ-centered approach playing out in modern life? How does this affect the people of your parish, especially young people? How do you describe the Christ-centered approach in your own words?

[45] How do you experience the interaction of conscience with church law? What has been your experience of a wrongly formed conscience? When might this happen? How easily are we humans fooled by our desires or passions? How can an accompanist help us avoid this, or how could you as an accompanist to others help someone avoid the pitfall of a rashly formed conscience?

Accompaniment toward discernment

AN INTRODUCTION AND FOUR PRINCIPLES

PRAYER
Become aware of the presence of God

ALL: In the name of the Father, and of the Son,
and of the Holy Spirit. Amen.

[1] As we accompany one another, we become Christ for one another, opening up together the mysteries of life and faith. With the patience and kindness of Christ, we allow each other to sort out the complex situations of our lives and follow a pathway that leads to holiness and wholeness.

[2] "That same day two of them were walking to the village Emmaus, about seven miles out of Jerusalem. They were deep in conversation, going over all these things that had happened. In the middle of their talk and questions, Jesus came up and walked along with them" (Luke 24:13–15, The Message).

[3] Let us become aware now of how Jesus walks with us. In the story of Emmaus in Luke's gospel, the encounter with the risen Jesus led, of course, to them breaking bread together. He was their accompanist. How do you experience Jesus accompanying you? How do you become

Christ for others as you accompany them? (*Brief sacred pause, followed by sharing.*)

[4] O God, we know that you are with us, and that you accompany us in all that we do. Grant that by the light of your Holy Spirit we may have the wisdom to accompany others well and the courage to take up this work. We pray through Christ, our Lord.

ALL: Amen.

INTRODUCTION
Listening deeply for the voice of Jesus

[5] As we learn the art of accompaniment toward discernment, we realize that, when we listen to our conscience, we are listening to God. In order to discern God's voice amid the clamor of other noisy voices in our hearts, we must learn how to sort them out. The din of voices in modern life is deafening. How can we trust that it is God's voice we hear?

[6] Elijah faced this same question. Do you recall his story? Elijah felt a God-given inner urge to go out and stand on a high mountain before the Lord. He knew the Lord was calling him and he was listening intently for the Lord's voice. We are the same in our desire to hear God speaking and to discern his voice; we, too, stand and listen.

[7] So it was with Elijah as he stood there listening. "Now there was a great wind," the text tells us. It was "so strong that it was splitting mountains...but the Lord was not in the wind; and after the wind an earthquake, but the Lord was not in the earthquake; and after the earthquake a fire, but the Lord was not in the fire; and after the fire, a sound of sheer silence" (1 Kings 19:11–12, NRSV).

[8] Sheer silence. When Elijah heard this silence "he wrapped his face in his mantle and went out and stood at the entrance of the cave" (13a). And it was then and there that he heard God's voice. The first step in discernment, then, is to listen as God speaks in the silence of our hearts, and this requires a life that includes some quiet and alone time for self-examination and introspection.

[9] Listening to God also requires a willingness to be accompanied toward discernment. We are called to practice such discernment throughout our lives. Even for those who are steeped in spirituality and religious practice this idea must be emphasized and repeated often. We tend to lapse into a sort of spiritual auto-pilot—accepting the status quo in our lifestyles and choices—often without returning to the Lord to be refreshed and renewed.

IN YOUR OWN WORDS (DISCUSSION TIME)

[10] What is your experience of hearing God in the silence of your heart? How has God spoken in your own life? How do you think members of the parish hear God's voice? What is it like to listen for God's voice but hear nothing?

PRINCIPLE #1
Discernment deals with practical, life-changing questions

[11] When we accompany others, one of the keys to success is that we clearly identify the decision to be made or the issue to be resolved in the life of the one being accompanied. Vague questions or unease don't contain within them a clear enough question for discernment. Therefore, the first principle is that the matter being discerned should be practical. It should be about doing or not doing something. It has to be real; that is, there really must be a decision called for. The accompanist should challenge the ones being accompanied to clarify this.

[12] Furthermore, one cannot discern something for which he or she doesn't have the right to choose. For example, one cannot discern about something that someone else is doing, or about something we want them to do. The matter must be one over which we have at least a little control and about which the ones being accompanied can get the information needed to make a clear choice.

[13] In accompanying others the issue or question should be clearly articulated and phrased. The words chosen to discuss the question are very important. Again, vague statements or assumptions don't serve accompaniment and discernment very well. Guide the ones being accompanied to state the question in a concrete way. What precise choice do the ones being accompanied face and what is the alternative? Toward what do the ones being accompanied think God may be drawing them?

PRINCIPLE #2
Discernment is couched in prayer

[14] Accompanists help the ones being accompanied to pray that their hearts may be open to following God's desire and will. Help the ones being accompanied to focus their hearts on the presence of Jesus who stands beside us every day. In prayer, help the ones being accompanied to let go of any sort of prejudice or judgment that could cloud how God speaks to them.

[15] As you accompany other persons in this prayer discuss what stands in the way of freedom for them. Are there past hurts? Is there self-pity or selfishness? Do the ones being accompanied suffer from indifference? Ask Jesus to remove any habits or obstacles such as fear, anger, aggression, or perfectionism.

[16] Prayer of this sort may take place over several days or weeks. Guide the ones being accompanied to place the matter "at the back of their

minds" and ask God to help them attend to it as the right moments come along. They may awake in the night with insights or they may find peace on a quiet walk with a friend. Help them to be aware of the words and stories of Jesus in the gospels. The teachings of Jesus become our principal guide.

[17] Encourage the ones being accompanied to "chat" frankly and informally with Jesus about this. Teach them to ask for freedom and detachment; to ask for an open heart to embrace whatever they're being called to do. Above all, guide them to become intimate with Jesus in their prayer. Ask for deep love: love for God, for the people who will be affected by the decision, and for themselves and their families. Ask that any obstacle in their heart may be removed so that they can do what the Holy Spirit is leading them to.

PRINCIPLE #3
Discernment eventually leads to a discussion of the matter

[18] At some point along the way, there must be a formal discussion about the matter at hand. A time will come when you are ready to talk through all the pros and cons, the person's values, motives, and desires. This formal discussion may take place in a very informal setting as you accompany the other, and there may be several discussions over a period of weeks or months. If the decision is not a major one, this may quickly lead to a choice. If it is life-changing, more time may be required.

[19] The *Catechism* instructs us to discern our conscience in article 1785, and it sets the method for this principle. "In the formation of conscience," it says, "the Word of God is the light for our path; we must assimilate it in faith and prayer and put it into practice. We must also examine our conscience before the Lord's Cross. We are assisted by the gifts of the Holy Spirit, aided by the witness or advice of others and guided by the authoritative teaching of the Church."

[20] As we said in statement number 16 above, an accompanist helps those being guided to consult the word of God and to do so in an ongoing way. Accompany them to think about the gospel stories, imagining themselves as part of each one and allowing God to grant them insight and vision. God will reveal his desire for them slowly as they encounter Scripture again and again. Thus, a good accompanist helps the ones being accompanied to assimilate the word of God and put it into practice.

[21] Returning to article 1785 of the *Catechism*, we are reminded that the Lord's cross is the single central image that leads the ones being accompanied to truly hear their calling. In what way are they called to die to themselves? How are they called to take up their own cross and follow Jesus? What sacrifices and difficulties are they called to bear for the sake of the kingdom of God? How does their awareness of the plight of "the least among us" call them to the practice of self-giving love?

[22] Through this prayer they are indeed "assisted by the gifts of the Holy Spirit." As we said above, an accompanist helps the ones being accompanied to be open to the Spirit. It is the Spirit speaking in our hearts to whom we must listen. The Spirit often speaks to us as we imagine ourselves present with Jesus, listening to his parables, witnessing and responding to the wonders of his works, and having one-on-one time with him.

[23] Returning again to article 1785, we know that the very process of accompaniment is itself "the witness and advice of others," which the *Catechism* teaches is so important. Not every accompanist is fully capable of guiding others through every situation that may arise, so a plan for accompaniment must include a way for those accompanying others to refer people to the priest or to professional counselors if needed—and to know when this is appropriate.

[24] And here in this step we also consider the teaching of the church regarding our question. The accompanist must be ready to allow the

ones being accompanied to be "guided by the authoritative teaching of the Church" without prejudice or judgment. We hold up the church's law and teaching as the norm, inviting the ones being accompanied to respond with good faith to that.

[25] To conclude our treatment of this principle, then, the accompanist helps the ones being accompanied to bring all these factors into a formal discussion, to talk through the pros and cons, and to reconcile themselves to church teaching. The accompanist must be careful in this step to avoid imposing his or her point of view onto the one being accompanied. God is acting in this person's life, and our reverence for that mystery must guide us to allow them to respond to God, not to us.

[26] The accompanist must practice his or her own discernment during this process. The accompanist must continue to keep his or her own heart in prayer. The accompanist must hold the ones being accompanied before the Lord in love, paying attention to anything that may prejudice their role as their coach and guide. Accompanists cannot coach others if they aren't themselves constantly standing before the Lord.

PRINCIPLE #4
Good decisions made in discernment lead to consolation

[27] And finally, a conclusion is reached. You cannot go on discerning forever. In simple matters, the conclusion may be reached within a matter of hours. In more complex matters, over more time. If the one being accompanied has come to the Lord with honesty and humility, you will both begin to see a direction and decision emerge. If this clear choice does not emerge, continue to pray, talk, and listen. Help the person pay attention to inner movements from one option to another. Eventually, he or she will focus on one or another alternative.

[28] As the decision is reached and the choice made, the accompanist

invites the person to turn to Jesus within his or her heart and ask God for feelings of consolation, a sense of rightness, and peace. When one's desires and decisions are clearly drawn from and toward God, this sense of well-being and consolation emerges. The one being accompanied may feel a new freedom and a sense of relief at having landed on the right direction.

[29] The feelings that accompany consolation are happiness, satisfaction at having chosen well, enthusiasm for the choice, love for God, courage to move in the direction of the decision, and trust in God's voice echoing in his or her conscience. If consolation and its related feelings does not emerge, then in all likelihood the discernment was not complete and you must accompany him or her further down the pathway.

[30] We humans all have the right to act according to a carefully formed conscience. We must not be forced to act contrary to our conscience, nor must we be prevented from following it, especially in religious matters (*Catechism*, 1782).

[31] "A human being," the *Catechism* reminds us in article 1790, "must always obey the certain judgment of his [or her] conscience." To act deliberately against our conscience is to condemn ourselves. As Cardinal Cupich puts it, "If people come to a decision in good conscience, then our job is to help them move forward and to respect that. The conscience is inviolable and we have to respect that when they make decisions…" (Interview at Vatican Press Office, Oct 16, 2015).

[32] In the end, our conscience is enlightened by faith and driven by charity. The more we follow our conscience in all things, the more we grow to be persons of intentional love and not blind choice (*Catechism*, 1794).

IN YOUR OWN WORDS (DISCUSSION TIME)
[33] What do you find hopeful in this discussion? What do you find trou-

bling? Discuss ways in which these principles could change the way you teach, preach, or counsel others. What experiences have you had related to the proper formation of conscience?

Hallmarks of an "Accompanying Parish"

NINE HALLMARKS FOR USE IN PASTORAL PLANNING

PRAYER

Become aware of the presence of God

ALL: In the name of the Father, and of the Son, and of the Holy Spirit. Amen.

[1] The ministry of accompaniment is one that we take up now as pastoral leaders and ministers, as parents and spouses, or as friends and neighbors. As we come to understand this way of walking with each other in life, we come to see that, through us, God touches the hearts of those near us.

[2] "We have not ceased praying for you and asking that you may be filled with the knowledge of God's will in all spiritual wisdom and understanding, so that you may lead lives worthy of the Lord, fully pleasing to him, as you bear fruit in every good work and as you grow in the knowledge of God" (Colossians 1:9b–10, NRSV).

[3] Let us become consciously aware now of how God is present to each of us individually as we move through each day. The grace or power of God gives us insight, spiritual wisdom, and understanding. How do you experience this grace in your own life? Turn your heart toward God now

and ask for an open heart so that you might grow in your knowledge of God. (*Brief sacred pause, followed by sharing.*)

[4] O God, we know that you are with us, and that you accompany us in all that we do. We open our hearts to your love. Grant that, by the light of your Holy Spirit, we may be humble as we walk with others and charitable in all that we do here today. We pray through Christ, our Lord.

ALL: Amen.

HALLMARK #1
The parish priest and pastoral team are committed to accompaniment

[5] An "accompanying parish" is one in which the pastor and pastoral team intentionally portray a particular attitude and posture toward all members of the parish, both the active as well as the less active. The attitude is one of understanding that people respond only as much as they are able to, and the posture is one of acceptance, love, and patience.

[6] To decide to become an accompanying parish is a decision to have reverence for each person's journey and, while clearly announcing the norms of church law, to allow each person to meet those norms gradually as they are able. In such a parish, as Pope Francis teaches, every effort is made to encourage the development of an enlightened conscience formed by serious discernment, led by the pastor and pastoral team (*The Joy of Love*, 303).

[7] In an accompanying parish the team understands that "conscience can do more than recognize that a given situation does not correspond objectively to the overall demands of the Gospel. *It can also recognize with sincerity and honesty what for now is the most generous response which can be given to God, and come to see with a certain moral security*

that it is what God himself is asking amid the concrete complexity of one's limits, while yet not fully the objective ideal" (*The Joy of Love*, 303, emphasis mine).

[8] To merely enforce the church's law is simply not enough. One can follow the law precisely and still be in serious, mortal sin. For example, in the matter of sexual relations, it is permitted under the law for couples properly married in the church. But even for such a couple sexual relations could be manipulative, violent, or coercive. Within marriage, sexual relations could even be rape! That it's legal does not make it loving. Hence, much more is required than merely keeping the letter of the law.

[9] In an accompanying parish, therefore, while the ideal of church law is upheld and taught, it is not used to judge, condemn, or exclude anyone from God's love, God's family, or the grace of sharing in community. The parish does not, in other words, become church-law-centered. Beyond that, such a parish is also careful not to portray an attitude of self-centered formation under the rubrics of which pretty much any decision or choice is honored as holy.

[10] In between those extremes an accompanying parish balances its message and teaching, its tone and tenor, by centering it on Christ and his pedagogy. In such a parish, people are taught to pray, to turn their hearts to Christ and the saints, to be open to the Holy Spirit. They are given help to discern what is going on in their respective consciences, always with an ear to the teachings of Jesus.

[11] Such a parish is able to integrate into parish life again even those whose marriages have led them to divorce and civil remarriage or cohabitation. "The logic of integration is the key to their pastoral care, a care which would allow them not only to realize that they belong to the Church as the body of Christ, but also to know that they can have a joyful and fruitful experience in it" (*The Joy of Love*, 299).

IN YOUR OWN WORDS (DISCUSSION TIME)

[12] Evaluate your own parish approach to accompaniment. How well understood do you think it is, first among members of the team and key volunteers, and second, among the people as a whole? What is the tone and tenor of "the message" your parish sends to people through announcements, the welcome people get at the reception desk, homilies, program structures, and so forth?

HALLMARK #2

The parish team plans for ways to increase accompaniment

[13] Accompaniment is not a practice that can be applied successfully on a piecemeal basis in a parish. If two members of the parish team are enthusiastic about a Christ-centered approach to discernment and formation but two others want to either be church-law-centered (and thereby enforce the rules literally) or be individual-centered (and adopt an "anything goes" approach), a pastoral and muddy mess results.

[14] Pope Francis is asking the parishes of the church to learn the art of accompaniment, and the parish team must come together to embrace accompaniment as a pastoral strategy. Accompaniment must become the "theme song" of parish life. The tone of everything that is said in public within the parish, from the homilies to the announcements to the structure of programs, must reflect it. A parish, in other words, must decide to become an "accompanying parish."

[15] Accompaniment is not accidental in a parish. To succeed as an accompanying parish requires the pastor and parish team to sit down together and do some planning. In many parishes today, this will mean very little change. The pastoral team already has learned how to accompany folks on their journeys of faith. Patience and watchful love are already the stock and trade of everything from the sacrament of reconcilia-

tion to faith-formation programs. Everyone is welcomed to come in "just as they are" but also encouraged to grow in faith.

[16] Other parishes need small adjustments and evaluation in order to move into this direction. "At times we find it hard to make room for God's unconditional love in our pastoral activity," Pope Francis reminds us in *The Joy of Love*, 311. "We put so many conditions on mercy that we empty it of its concrete meaning and real significance," he said. For parish teams who find this difficult, the first steps may be to pray for openness to the Spirit.

[17] On the level of the universal church, Pope Francis has opened new doors for us who work on the local level in parish pastoral ministries. These open doors make becoming an accompanying parish possible. Without changing core teachings of the church, the Holy Father has refreshed pastoral ministry in order to make it less judgmental and more open to how God may be working in people's lives, even when we do not understand it.

[18] In doing this he sets out for us a pretty clear picture of what an accompanying parish might look like. Again, in all parish activities and messages the theme song of accompaniment must be audible to all.

HALLMARK #3
Mercy for people's life situations is obvious and generous

[19] One of the doors he has opened is the doorway of mercy. "We have learned that God bends down to us (cf. Hos 11:4)," Pope Francis said in *Mercy and Misery*, 16, "so that we may imitate him in bending down to our brothers and sisters." Many people, he said, want to return to the church. We in parish ministry are the ones who will receive and welcome them. We must "bend down" to meet them where they are.

[20] "The [recent] Jubilee Year…has set us on a new pathway in this regard and it is the way of charity. We are called to joyfully offer charity to all who come to us. It is the road of mercy, on which we meet so many of our brothers and sisters who reach out for someone to take their hand and become a companion on the way" (*Mercy and Misery*, 16).

[21] Mercy, as Pope Francis said in article 10 of the bull *The Face of Mercy*, is the work of the church. We do not need any further permission from him or anyone to proceed to build a church of mercy. Pope Francis speaks of this with urgency in his words.

[22] Not only must each parish be merciful to all, but we must be the witness to the world. All who look on us should see and understand God's mercy and learn to practice it by watching us. We are a light to the world, one that announces that God loves us and that we love each other.

HALLMARK #4
Families are accompanied in the religious education programs

[23] In a parish accompanying people with mercy the leaders learn how to accompany each family who is part of the religious education program. Many of these families are not at Mass on the weekend, but we continue to reach out to them, to invite them to participate more fully, and to show them our love.

[24] Many families struggle to keep up with all the various deadlines, rules, and requirements of the program. To the leaders, these all seem reasonable and necessary, but to many families they are quite difficult. In particular, single-parent homes and ecumenical families, where only one parent is juggling competing demands, may be most in need of our mercy. For the leaders, this means special sacrifices are needed. We must give up our rigidity and become more flexible.

[25] In an accompanying parish, parents are coached to form their own children but always in the context of parish gatherings. They are equipped to accompany their own children through these early stages of life and faith. And for those parents who are not Catholic, a special welcome is offered to help them feel included, to help them understand what their children are learning, and to demonstrate God's love for and radical acceptance of them.

HALLMARK #5
Everyone is accompanied through the Sunday liturgy

[26] In a parish of mercy and accompaniment leaders offer a welcome and outstretched hand to everyone who joins in the assembly for liturgy, including those many who do not feel welcome there now. As a merciful community, leaders actually plan how to reach out to the many households who are absent or only present infrequently, to make sure they feel welcome and not judged.

[27] To those many people not currently at the parish table due to an irregular marriage, leaders offer accompaniment to help them bring their situation to the matrimonial tribunal, to the priest in confession, or to a place where they are right with their own conscience.

[28] Likewise at Sunday liturgy in an accompanying parish, a special word is offered to non-Catholic spouses and friends of the parishioners to welcome them in Christ's name, make them feel at home, and help them learn how we celebrate the liturgy.

[29] But for all Catholics, whether in stable, approved marriages or not, whether single people, members of religious communities, or strangers dropping in on a spiritual search, the tone, tenor, and terminology used in the liturgy is inclusive, respectful, and Christ-centered. Nothing we do

at the parish is more important than this. Everyone present leaves feeling the force of grace that the liturgy offers to all.

[30] This begins with the greeting at the front door, continues into the opening rites, is extended and celebrated in the liturgies of Word and Eucharist, and goes out the door with the send-off, the coffee hour, and the bulletin. Every dimension of liturgical life sees itself as designed to accompany everyone to understand more fully the amazing forgiveness, love, and real presence of Christ.

HALLMARK #6
Pastoral care ministers are "accompaniment specialists"

[31] In a parish of mercy and accompaniment, the pastoral care work of the parish may become one of the most vital ways in which accompaniment occurs. Leaders learn how to insert practices of mercy into pastoral care and outreach ministries, including welcoming people to various activities even if they are not welcome to receive communion at Mass.

[32] They offer the sick and dying special mercy and accompaniment to achieve healing or a peaceful death in Christ. They seek out the inactive members of the parish one-by-one to say once again to them, "We are the People of God and you are part of our family. We welcome you regardless your situation in life."

[33] In an accompanying parish, leaders reach out to people who live near the parish church but are not in our religious community. They may be Protestant, Muslim, Jewish, Hindu, or of no faith at all, but they are children of God. We are also called to accompany these neighbors and assist them as needs arise.

[27] Likewise, the poor of our neighborhoods, nation, and the world. To these we have been given a special calling since whatever we do for

them we do for Christ himself. "This entails appreciating the poor in their goodness, in their experience of life, in their culture, and in their ways of living the faith...The poor person, when loved, 'is esteemed as of great value...' Only on the basis of this real and sincere closeness can we properly accompany the poor on their path of liberation. Only this will ensure that 'in every Christian community the poor feel at home'" (*The Joy of the Gospel,* 199).

HALLMARK #7
The "voice" of the parish is consistently companionable

[28] In an accompanying parish, leaders pay special attention to the office hours of the parish, as well as the schedule when the doors of the church are open and unlocked. Can everyone manage to fit their needs into the parish office hours? Are the office hours arranged for the convenience of the team or of the people?

[29] Attention is also paid to the front desk and who sits there; to the potential that a clubby feeling could emerge among those who know each other well in the parish and are long-time members; to the parish phones and the automatic answering systems, which can leave people feeling unattended to, especially if English is not their first language; to the web site and social media pages; and to how accessible are the parish priests and team members.

[30] Each of these elements of parish life demonstrates our care for the people. The "voice" or constant message of the parish should be, "We are here for you. We do not judge you or your situation in life. You can trust us to accompany you to healing, inclusion, the sacraments, and faith formation. Whatever has happened in your life, we do not condemn you. You belong to us because you belong to Christ."

HALLMARK #8
The parish respects that people gradually become fully faithful

[31] Another doorway that Pope Francis has opened for us is one to which Pope St. John Paul II first introduced us: the law of gradualness in pastoral ministry. We grow able to know, love, and do moral good gradually. Little by little as we mature in faith, we become more able to carry out the demands of the law.

[32] "For the law is itself a gift of God which points out the way" and this gift is given to everyone. We are able to follow the law only with the help of grace. As we embrace God's love and endless forgiveness, we become gradually more able to allow this love to transform our lives (*The Joy of Love*, 295). So rather than being church-law-centered and imposing the same law on every situation, we allow people to gradually grow toward the ideal of that law.

[33] "For this reason, a pastor [or pastoral team member] cannot feel that it is enough simply to apply moral laws to those living in 'irregular' situations," Pope Francis teaches us, "as if they were stones to throw at people's lives. This would bespeak the closed heart of one used to hiding behind the Church's teachings..." (*The Joy of Love*, 305).

[34] Instead, accompaniment suggests we get to know people whose marriages don't quite measure up to our laws, whether gay or straight. We get to know people who are making choices about regulating when to become pregnant, how to manage their relative wealth, what to think about the death penalty, how to welcome immigrants into their country, and so forth.

[35] Regardless their choices, we welcome them, help them see that we do not judge them, and love them sincerely in their present moment. Only then can we help them grow gradually into a faithful lifestyle and

set of choices. Not everyone can be fully faithful at every moment and this includes those parish or church leaders who demand it of others.

HALLMARK #9
The parish reaches out beyond its comfort zone

[36] Another doorway that Pope Francis has opened is laced into all his teaching. He wants us out on the streets where the people are and live. "Let us go forth...to offer everyone the life of Jesus Christ. I prefer a Church which is bruised, hurting and dirty because it has been out on the streets," Pope Francis has repeatedly said, "rather than a Church which is unhealthy from being confined and from clinging to its own security" (*The Joy of the Gospel*, 49).

[37] This is how we evangelize each other as well as those who are presently inactive Catholics. "An evangelizing community gets involved by word and deed in people's daily lives; it bridges distances, it is willing to abase itself if necessary, and it embraces human life, touching the suffering flesh of Christ in others.

[38] "Evangelizers thus take on the 'smell of the sheep' and the sheep are willing to hear their voice. An evangelizing community is also supportive, standing by people at every step of the way, no matter how difficult or lengthy this may prove to be" (*The Joy of the Gospel*, 24).

[39] It isn't enough to sit back in our parish offices and wait for people to come to us. Too many have felt the sting of our judgments in the past, too many the pain of rejection. For many people, when they came to us asking for bread, we offered them only a stone. They are absent now, and for many, their faith has grown cold. But rather than spending our time analyzing and judging them for this, Pope Francis wants us to reach out anew and welcome them home.

[40] "It is a matter of reaching out to everyone," he said in *The Joy of Love* #297, "of needing to help each person find his or her proper way of participating in the ecclesial community and thus to experience being touched by an 'unmerited, unconditional and gratuitous' mercy." He reminds us that no one should be condemned forever because that suggests that we have lost hope in God's mercy.

[41] When he makes this forceful point in *The Joy of Love*, 297, he very clearly lets us know about whom he is talking. "Here I am not speaking only of the divorced and remarried, but of everyone, in whatever situation they find themselves." This includes all whose lives have led them or who have been pushed by us, for whatever reason, away from the family of God.

[42] In all the work we do to accompany others, we should always remember what Pope Francis has taught us forcefully and repeatedly: we love others, we withhold judgment about them, and we act with mercy toward them. Why? Because God first loved us, and God's very name is mercy. As accompanists we learn to treat others in the same way that God constantly treats us. In the words of Pope Francis, we cannot forget that "mercy is not only the working of the Father; it becomes a criterion for knowing who his true children are. In a word, we are called to show mercy because mercy was first shown to us" (*The Joy of Love*, 310).

IN YOUR OWN WORDS (DISCUSSION TIME)

[43] What decision is your parish taking about becoming an accompanying parish? Who would object to becoming an accompanying and more merciful parish? What must change for this to become a reality in your parish? On what current strengths and leadership can you build?

[44] Even if they are not presently asking for our accompaniment because they have been judged, rejected, or condemned in the past by us, what groups of people are most in need of knowing God's mercy in their lives? How might you reach out to them now?

[45] Who are the people in our midst who yearn for our spiritual accompaniment? Using the hallmarks described in this final chapter (and please add your own to our list), how would you (1) evaluate your own parish, and (2) construct a parish plan to increase accompaniment?

Also Available

THE JOY OF LOVE
A Group Reading Guide to Pope Francis' Amoris Laetitia
BILL HUEBSCH

In this plain-English study guide, acclaimed scholar and theologian Bill Huebsch makes Pope Francis' message even more accessible, with paraphrased summaries of each article, and prayerful discussion and reflection questions that can help each of us see how Francis' words apply to our own lives.

64 PAGES | $4.95 (BULK PRICING AVAILABLE) | 9781627851985

ON CARE FOR OUR COMMON HOME
Group Reading Guide to Laudato Si'
BILL HUEBSCH

This encyclical, drawing its name from St. Francis' *Canticle of the Creatures*, reminds us that earth is our common home and that we must care for it. This guide offers a summary of every article in Pope Francis' groundbreaking document and a small group reflection process to help everyone read it and understand it. The six small group sessions outlined here include group reading, discussion, prayer, and action suggestions (for communal or personal use) making it ideal for youth ministry, confirmation programs, parish leaders, small communities, clergy groups, adult formation, the RCIA, or families.

48 PAGES | $3.50 (BULK PRICING AVAILABLE) | 9781627851220

THE JOY OF THE GOSPEL
A Group Reading Guide to Pope Francis' Evangelii Gaudium
BILL HUEBSCH

This in-plain-English study guide offers a paraphrased summary of every article in Pope Francis' recent document, with reflection/discussion questions for group or individual use.

48 PAGES | $3.50 (BULK PRICING AVAILABLE) | 9781627850193

TO ORDER CALL 1-800-321-0411
OR VISIT WWW.TWENTYTHIRDPUBLICATIONS.COM

TWENTY-THIRD PUBLICATIONS
A division of Bayard, Inc.